Presented to

_____

From

_____

Date

_____

THE
Victorian Lady

PAINTINGS BY

Alan Maley

TEXT BY

Janna C. Walkup

HARVEST HOUSE PUBLISHERS
EUGENE, OREGON

The Victorian Lady
Copyright © 1998 Harvest House Publishers
Eugene, Oregon 97402

All works of art contained in this book are copyrighted by Alan Maley and
reproduced under license from Pamela Maley. For more information
regarding art featured in this book, please contact:

>Past Impressions
>1191 Chess Drive, Suite C
>Foster City, CA 94404
>(800) 732-7332

Library of Congress Cataloging-in-Publication Data
Walkup, Janna, 1970-
    The Victorian lady / paintings by Alan Maley ; text by Janna
Walkup.
        p. cm.
    ISBN 1-56507-865-9
    1. Women—England—History—19th century.   2. Decorative arts,
Victorian.   3. Gardens, Victorian.   4. England—Social life and
customs—19th century.   5. Great Britain—History—Victoria,
1837-1901.   I. Maley, Alan, 1931-1995. II. Title.
HQ1596.W35 1998
305.4'0942—dc21   98-3264
                                                                 CIP

Design and production by Koechel Peterson & Associates, Minneapolis,
Minnesota

Printed in the United States of America.

98 99 00 01 02 03 04 05 06 07 / **IP** / 10 9 8 7 6 5 4 3 2 1

Contents

The Victorian Lady

The Victorian Lady

You feel her gracious personality in the way she welcomes callers, smiling a cheerful greeting, offering china cups of steaming tea, a plate of her deliciously rich raspberry tarts, and—the best welcome of all—her attentiveness to their lives. You see her patience and gentleness in the way she teaches and cares for her children, reading them their very first stories and creating new games to amuse and educate their quick, young minds. You hear her intelligence in her delightful conversation with others and in her sharing of her varied hobbies, as she discusses the latest in literature and science and tells of her progress in photography and oil-painting. Her charmingly decorated home, refreshing gardens, and fine style of dress all tell of her beauty, but the truest beauty comes from the Victorian lady's heart.

A woman of elegance and excellence, her sparkling eyes, merry laughter, and compassionate soul attest to who she is—a lady in the best sense of the word. She adores romance, takes pleasure in spontaneous adventures, and dearly cherishes her faith. She tends to the needs of others, taking baskets of food and other necessities to those less fortunate than herself. Her children and all of their chums find comfortable nooks in her kitchen, telling her their most interesting stories—real or make-believe, depending on the action of the day—in exchange for her amused reaction and a tasty treat. Ready for a new experience, she sets out on a fishing expedition or takes up the amusing new sport of bicycling.

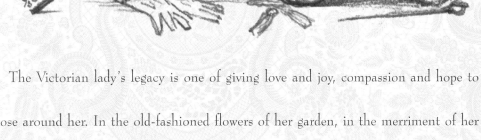

The Victorian lady's legacy is one of giving love and joy, compassion and hope to those around her. In the old-fashioned flowers of her garden, in the merriment of her much-anticipated afternoon teas, in her gentle whispers of love reserved only for her beloved, her virtues shine brightly.

Chapter One
THE COMFORTS OF HOME

She went into the drawing-room and lighted the fire; then, picking up the cushions, one by one, that Mary had disposed so carefully, she threw them back on to the chairs and the couches. That made all the difference; the room came alive at once.

—KATHERINE MANSFIELD, *Bliss*

Her home is, perhaps, a suburban villa—its sitting rooms filled with velvet sofas and chairs of royal elegance, with a shiny black grand piano in the parlor. Or she could live in a spacious house in the country, with lace draperies peeking from the multi-paneled windows and lively floral fabrics— beds of roses and hydrangeas, morning glories and snowdrops—dressing the fashionable furnishings. She might

make her home in a cozy thatch-roofed cottage, its charming outline kept secret by the climbing vines of ivy and clematis and the tumble of wildflowers that burst forth from the playful garden.

You might picture her best, though, in the traditional Victorian mansion, with its intricate gingerbread ornamentation and window boxes bursting with blooms. She is the Victorian lady, and her home reflects the creativity, serenity, and beauty she holds dear.

Winding her way through the gardens, arriving home from a morning of paying calls or an afternoon of picking apples in the orchard or gathering a bouquet of Queen Anne's lace for the tea table, she passes a wall of climbing roses, a cluster of terra-cotta pots overflowing with mint, and a delicate bed of pansies and alyssum. The garden path escorts her to an inviting porch, large enough for tea parties and luncheons in favorable weather. A decorative door—perhaps boasting stained-glass work or a perfectly ovalled pane of glass—sets off the pink geraniums and trailing blue lobelia in the window boxes, while robins and bluejays trill a welcome "hello."

Her eyes dwelt affectionately on Green Gables, peering through its network of trees and reflecting the sunlight back from its windows in several little coruscations of glory. Marilla, as she picked her steps along the damp lane, thought that it was really a satisfaction to know that she was going home to a briskly snapping wood fire and a table nicely spread for tea...

—LUCY MAUD MONTGOMERY, *ANNE OF GREEN GABLES*

The lady of the home designs each of her rooms with a specific purpose in mind—grand social occasions, gentle family times together, quiet moments spent in solitude, reflecting upon the day's happenings and anticipating future events. It is a welcoming home, full of the graceful details cherished so deeply by the Victorian woman.

The Front Entrance—A well-kept and comfortable front entrance is essential to a proper Victorian residence, as the lady of the home receives ever so many callers each day. The ideal hall is usually built quite narrow, the key furnishings being seats, mirrors, and a coat and hat rack for visitors. A card-receiver to hold calling cards, an umbrella stand, a small table to hold a becoming bouquet of flowers,

Colors of the Home

THE VICTORIAN LADY DELIGHTS IN CHOOSING FASHIONABLE AND EXQUISITE COLORS FOR THE EXTERIOR AND INDIVIDUAL ROOMS OF HER HOME. SOME OF HER FAVORED COLOR COMBINATIONS INCLUDE—

CREAM WHITE *and* TURKEY RED

BLUE *and* GREEN

CREAM *and* VIOLET

SALMON *and* CHOCOLATE *accented with* SAGE GREEN

PRIMROSE *and* DARK GREEN

PALE YELLOW *and* CHOCOLATE

MAROON *and* PALLID SEA GREEN

COWSLIP COLORS

A Well-Appointed Writing Desk

I went and sat down at the writing-desk, and I thought how strange it was that this room, so lovely, and so rich in colour, should be, at the same time, so business-like and purposeful.

—DAPHNE DU MAURIER, *REBECCA*

INVITATIONS TO SEND, ACCOUNTS TO SETTLE, CORRESPONDENCE TO ANSWER, SHOPPING LISTS TO PEN— THE VICTORIAN LADY MAKES EXCELLENT USE OF HER WRITING DESK, AND KEEPS IT WELL-STOCKED WITH ONLY THE BEST—

FINE WRITING PAPER *and* MATCHING ENVELOPES

WELL-CRAFTED INK PENS, DECORATIVE BOTTLES FILLED *with* INK, *and an* INKWELL

BLOTTERS, LETTER SEALS, *and* SEALING WAX

AN ERASING KNIFE *and a* LETTER OPENER MADE *of* SILVER

SMALL VASES FILLED *with* FRAGRANT FLOWERS

CANDLES *and* CANDLESTICKS

FAVORITE COLLECTIBLES *in* TINY NOOKS

PRIVATE JOURNALS *and* DIARIES

and a sturdy doormat are all simple but useful additions. A solid wood floor covered with attractive carpets imported from the East cradle weary feet and speak a soft welcome home.

The Parlor or Drawing Room—A special source of pride for the Victorian lady, the parlor (often referred to as the "drawing room") serves as the social center of her home. Here she hosts tea parties and musical evenings, and receives her callers. A piano or organ generally stands at attention in the center of the room, waiting for talented hands—quite often belonging to the lady of the house herself—to play a melody. The walls of the parlor—often covered with decorative wallpaper or painted an elegant hue—display well-grouped oil and watercolor paintings and prints. Cabinets hold collections of figurines, seashells, and fine china, and an array of plants and flowers bring the tranquillity of the outdoors into the room. Its windows dressed with elaborate lace, muslin, or velvet draperies, the parlor pampers its guests with comfortable sofas and chairs and elegant rugs and carpets.

The Dining Room—The entertaining sister of the parlor, the Victorian lady's dining room is the setting for her celebrated dinner parties, which often feature at least nine well-stocked courses. Dining room musts include a large table, perhaps crafted of fine

oak or mahogany, a matching set of chairs, light curtains, fresh floral arrangements, and a sideboard to hold the many dishes that comprise the feast. If space permits, satiated guests may recline in sofas and oversized chairs conveniently located in the dining room following the meal.

> It was a rosy room, hung with one of the new
> English chintzes, which also covered the deep sofa,
> and the bed with its rose-lined pillow-covers.
> —EDITH WHARTON, *NEW YEAR'S DAY*

The Library—Good books, plush rugs, and luxurious chairs and sofas. These are the essentials of a proper library. A window seat to catch the sun's rays and a fireplace for cold winter evenings add an ample dose of coziness to the austere study atmosphere.

The Conservatory—Potted palms, exotic orchids, and comfortable furnishings crafted of white wicker, with soft cushions in the shades and patterns of sky and gardens, turn the Victorian lady's conservatory into an ideal room for afternoon gatherings in summertime.

*She was so thankful for the softness of her
lavender-fragrant bed, and so delighted with the lovely
freshness of her chintz-hung room. As she lay upon her
pillow, she could see the boughs of the trees, and hear
the chatter of darting starlings. When her morning tea
was brought, it seemed like nectar to her.*

—FRANCES HODGSON BURNETT, *EMILY FOX-SETON*

The Breakfast Parlor and Kitchen—The
Victorian lady's breakfast parlor, though still
fashionably appointed, is substantially scaled
down from the kingly proportions of the dining room. The kitchen, though certainly func-
tional, is a creative refuge of its own with a
large center island for mixing and chopping, a
hearth for baking bread, and white wainscoting
and panoramic windows for airy refreshment.
Popular kitchen colors include creams, earthy
reds, and bronze greens, reflecting the copper
pots and pans and fine ceramic ware.

The Bedchamber—A brass or iron bed, often
canopied with lace draperies and covered in
linen sheets and faded cotton quilts, provides
the perfect backdrop to a romantic retreat.
Along with a bureau, table, easy chair, and
armoire, the Victorian lady fills her bedroom
with the flowers and photos that speak deepest
to her heart.

The Washroom—With a curved clawfoot tub
in iron or porcelain, a charming washstand
with a pitcher and bowl of lavender-scented
water resting atop, decorative ceramic tiles,
and piles of towels next to baskets of perfumed
French soaps and sachets, the Victorian lady's
washroom leaves no detail unattended in creating an oasis of purity and beauty.

*This was a woman's room, graceful, fragile, the room
of someone who had chosen every article of furniture
with great care, so that each chair, each vase, each
small, infinitesimal thing should be in harmony with
one another, and with her own personality.*

—DAPHNE DU MAURIER, *REBECCA*

The Essential Touches

Embroidered table linens and tasseled pillows. Specially chosen collections of smooth river stones and old-fashioned footstools full of character. A lovingly arranged grouping of family photographs—some quite likely taken by the lady herself—and decorated lampshades. Hand-painted fire screens and intricately stenciled wall designs. The Victorian domain showcases the inspired creativity of its mistress.

Along with her creative pursuits and decorating endeavors, the Victorian lady faithfully adheres to her own "to-do" list of domestic responsibilities. In the springtime she puts up light summer curtains and places airy cotton or muslin summer covers on the furniture. Come autumn, she has the chimney swept to prepare for cozy evenings by the fireside, and dresses the windows and furnishings in warm, dark fabrics—rich green or port velvet and heavy tapestry florals. Baking bread, harvesting fruits and vegetables, making jam, canning vegetables, drying fruit, and baking desserts make up her culinary pursuits.

The small frills and bobbles, ornaments and accessories of her home are set off by larger areas of detail—ceilings painted with exotic birds and nature scenes, luxurious Turkish rugs whispering secrets of faraway lands, stately grandfather clocks storing up memories with each reassuring *tick, tock*. The essential touches of a home, great and small.

Stay, stay at home, my heart, and rest,
Home-keeping hearts are happiest.
—HENRY WADSWORTH LONGFELLOW

But what on earth is half so dear—
So longed for—as the hearth of home?
—EMILY BRONTË, *A LITTLE WHILE*

Chapter Two
DEEP IN THE GARDENS

October though it was, the garden was still very sweet with dear,
old-fashioned unworldly flowers and shrubs—sweet may, southern-wood,
lemon verbena, alyssum, petunias, marigolds, and chrysanthemums.
—LUCY MAUD MONTGOMERY, *ANNE OF THE ISLAND*

Take a leisurely ramble through the gardens of the Victorian home. Note the tidy boxwood hedges, the kitchen gardens brimming with savory herbs and vegetables ready to be popped into a hearty soup, the perennial flower borders that surround the house and bring new surprises with each passing season, the orchards with trees laden heavy with peaches and cherries, perfectly ripe and juicy. Wander the stepping-stone path through the flower beds, some geometrically shaped with plants precisely placed, others carefree and wild in a cheerful commotion of colors and varieties.

Spend time alone in a private corner of the garden, deep in contemplation. Or mingle with other well-dressed guests at the social event of the summer—the garden party. Welcome to the Victorian woman's gardens, the outdoor rooms of her house, carpeted in green velvet and furnished with floral finery.

The wide carpet of turf that covered the level
hilltop seemed but the extension of a luxurious interior.
The great still oaks and beeches flung down a shade
as dense as that of velvet curtains; and the place was
furnished, like a room, with cushioned seats,
with rich-coloured rugs, with the books and
papers that lay on the grass.
—HENRY JAMES, *THE PORTRAIT OF A LADY*

The first flowers of the season, the tiny crocuses dressed in their cheery lilac and lemon-yellow best, nudge up through the snow, opening their petals tentatively. Soon they are joined by delicate white snowdrops, bright yellow jonquils, jewel-colored tulips, and fragrant pastel hyacinths. When these flowers come calling, the Victorian lady welcomes them into her garden as if they were princesses, attending to their every need and offering them places of honor in her home.

As spring turns to summer, the brilliant show in her borders, beds, and window boxes continues, with the new display featuring lively geraniums and fuchsias along with soft-spoken primroses, violas, and forget-me-nots. Bowers of roses, climbing clematis, and towering sunflowers help anchor the old-fashioned favorites—hollyhocks, sweet peas, foxglove, delphinium, phlox, and Canterbury bells.

The autumn palette reflects the bronze, orange, and golden hues of the falling leaves and setting sun—marigolds, chrysanthemums, and late summer sunflowers.

...the branches of purple and white lilac—the floating golden tressed laburnum boughs. Besides these, there were stately white lilies, sacred to the Virgin—hollyhocks, fraxinella, monk's-hood, pansies, primroses; every flower which blooms profusely in charming old-fashioned country-gardens was there...

—ELIZABETH GASKELL, *RUTH*

Gardens with Themes

THE OLD-FASHIONED GARDEN

SUNFLOWERS, HOLLYHOCKS, SWEET PEAS,
FOXGLOVES, DELPHINIUM, PHLOX, CANTERBURY BELLS,
CARNATIONS, COLUMBINES, MORNING GLORIES.

THE SCENTED GARDEN

ROSES, HONEYSUCKLE, LILACS, LABERNUM,
CLEMATIS, JASMINE, FOUR O'CLOCKS, PINKS,
CARNATIONS, PHLOX, LAVENDER.

THE WILDFLOWER COTTAGE GARDEN

CORNFLOWERS, BABY'S BREATH, LARKSPUR,
QUEEN ANNE'S LACE, JOHNNY JUMP-UPS, FORGET-ME-NOTS,
FOXGLOVES, MOUNTAIN GARLANDS.

THE KITCHEN GARDEN

CARROTS, LETTUCE, CUCUMBERS,
CHERRY TOMATOES, PARSLEY, BASIL, CHIVES,
CATMINT, LEMON BALM, SAGE, ROSEMARY, THYME,
LAVENDER, NASTURTIUMS, ORANGE MINT.

THE BUTTERFLY GARDEN

LARKSPUR, CORNFLOWERS, ALYSSUM,
LUPINE, COSMOS, PHLOX, DAISIES, PINCUSHION FLOWERS,
COLUMBINES, SUNFLOWERS.

Other areas of the garden are pleasing to eye and palate alike. The Victorian lady plants her kitchen garden with great care, making sure it is conveniently located near the back door and filling it to overflowing with her favorite vegetables—tomatoes, beans, potatoes, carrots, and peppers—and herbs—lemon thyme, lavender, rosemary, sage, dill, and chives. She'll have to walk deeper into the garden to reach the orchards, but the crisp apples and flavorful peaches will be well worth her walk. And along the path back to the house, she takes a moment to fill her basket with strawberries, currants, and gooseberries.

Like the Victorian house, no Victorian garden would be quite complete without the imaginative details that transform an ordinary space into a haven that renews spirit and soul. Besides residing in the usual beds and borders, flowers, herbs, and vegetables find themselves quite content in window boxes, clay and ceramic pots and vases, and wire hanging baskets. The Victorian lady furnishes her outdoor rooms with sundials, cast-iron garden seats, and wooden benches that complement the home's verandas, trellises, and porches.

When the weather is fine—and sometimes she ventures outdoors even when it's not, especially if she has a sturdy umbrella—the lady of the house will linger in her outdoor rooms, exploring their hidden corners and arranging them to her liking, drawing peace from the serene creation.

*The old lime-tree walk was like green cloisters, the very shadows
of the cherry-trees and apple-trees were heavy with fruit, the gooseberry-bushes were
so laden that their branches arched and rested on the earth, the strawberries and raspberries
grew in like profusion, and the peaches basked by the hundred on the wall.*

—CHARLES DICKENS, *BLEAK HOUSE*

*The warm-blue breathings of a hidden hearth
Broke from a bower of vine and honeysuckle.*

—ALFRED, LORD TENNYSON

Please Come to My Garden Party

Garden-parties are of every description, from the grand reception which finishes up with illuminations and dancing, to the quiet little afternoon spent in the modest grounds of some tiny suburban villa. They are generally given in the months of July and August, when the flowers are in their fullest beauty. In consequence of the variability of the English climate, it is impossible to send out the invitations very early, say more than a fortnight beforehand, and even then it is advisable to have the house prepared for emergencies, so that the entertainment may not be an entire fiasco in case of rain.

"There is something about old-fashioned mansions, built as this is, and old-fashioned gardens, that is especially delightful."
"I like everything old-fashioned," said Eleanor; "old-fashioned things are so much the honestest."

—ANTHONY TROLLOPE, *BARCHESTER TOWERS*

Invitations

Garden-party invitations are sent out on large invitation-cards, similar to those used for afternoon parties:

Mrs. Butterworth
At Home
from 4 to 8,

...or from 5 till 12, as the case may be, the nature of the entertainment being explained by the words "Garden-Party" being written in the right-hand corner of the card. Answers are expected, as to all other invitations, so that the hostess may know how many she has to provide for. The family is usually scattered about the grounds, so as to be able to pay attention to the different guests. The hostess or one of her daughters remains in the drawing-room, where the people are shown on entering. Some houses are so arranged that the hostess can receive her visitors upon a terrace leading into the garden, and this is pleasanter work than being tied to the house on a boiling summer's day. The people who stay in the house to receive the visitors certainly have a very dull time of it, as they are completely cut off from the scene of action!

❧ Strawberries

Tents are put up on the various lawns for refreshments, which consist of tea and coffee, and cakes and ices, but more especially fruit. A garden-party is nothing without strawberries, and if much money is laid out on any part of the entertainment it should be in the department of fruit.

❧ A Pretty Toilette

A garden-party presents a favorable opportunity for the display of a pretty toilette, and simplicity should be the prevailing idea of dress, whether it be a costly one or otherwise. Cool-looking muslins will have a happier effect than the most expensive material, and you should be careful that your dress does not look like an evening one done up to serve the day. A hat always looks well at a garden-party, but bonnets are more suitable to married ladies.

With regard to the etiquette of politeness at a garden-party, always be careful to find your hostess both on entering and leaving, and for the rest, enjoy yourself and look as happy as possible!

—*THE ETIQUETTE OF POLITENESS*

The Garden Party yesterday at Holland House was very nice. The house and gardens are too lovely. Betty and I wandered into the different rooms...We spent the rest of the time eating nectarines and strawberries.

—LADY EMILY LUTYENS, *A BLESSED GIRL*

Chapter Three
A PASTIME FOR EVERY SEASON

Boot, saddle, to horse, and away!

—ROBERT BROWNING

Indulging in her favorite pastimes and hobbies, the Victorian lady flings herself wholeheartedly into playing sports and games and pursuing her intellectual and artistic interests. Spring and summer bring outdoor pursuits, and when the crisp air of autumn and the chill of winter set in, she retreats to the well-appointed, comfortable rooms of her home to write and dream.

I had a delicious ride yesterday alone with Lady Anne through the most lovely woods where each turn seemed to bring us to something more beautiful than before.

—LADY EMILY LUTYENS, *A BLESSED GIRL*

Bicycling, tennis, croquet, cricket, golf—such a variety of amusing games to play! Croquet, when played with gentlemen, often becomes a game of flirtation for young ladies, as they tease and argue about the rules and playing methods of the genteel sport. The Victorian lady also invigorates herself with good exercise—riding (side saddle, if you please), walking, and hiking. Along with sunny summer days come lakeside outings in canoe or rowboat, archery parties on expansive lawns, and even adventurous fishing trips at a mountain river or stream.

In addition to sporting, the Victorian lady embarks upon other outings during the months of fair skies—shopping trips to the city, visits to zoos, fairs, public gardens, and pantomimes, dinners at great hotels, and trips to the theater may top her wish list of places to go. If she craves solitary time, she may wander fields and gardens, sketching wildflowers and writing poetry in a journal all her own. Or she may accompany a favored companion in a carriage ride through the park, with the two stopping to take photographs and share a picnic luncheon along the way.

There are so many good shops here....
One can step out of doors and get a thing in five minutes.

—JANE AUSTEN, *NORTHANGER ABBEY*

To cleave the air as though on wings,
defying time and space by putting what had been
a day's journey on foot behind one in a couple of hours!
Of passing garrulous acquaintances who had formerly held
one in one-sided conversation by the roadside for an hour, with a
light ting, ting *of the bell and a casual wave of recognition.*

—FLORA THOMPSON, WRITING ABOUT THE SPORT OF BICYCLING

The Marvelous Bicycle

SHE MAY LEARN FIRST ON A THREE-WHEELED TRICYCLE, THEN QUICKLY GRADUATE TO THE BICYCLE, THAT MARVELOUS CREATION THAT PERMITS ITS RIDER TO FLY DOWN HILLS AND OVER BRIDGES, COVERING THE COUNTRYSIDE IN A RUSH OF FRESH AIR, SKIRTS BILLOWING IN THE BREEZE. PERHAPS SHE HAS JOINED A BICYCLE CLUB, AND ACCOMPANIES THE GROUP ON THEIR MORNING OUTING, THEN SITS DOWN WITH THEM FOR A HEARTY TEA IN THE AFTERNOON. COME SUMMER THE GROUP WILL EMBARK UPON A WEEKEND BICYCLE TOUR OF THE COUNTRY, AND SHE WILL OUTFIT HERSELF IN THE PROPER ATTIRE FOR A LADY CYCLIST—A DARK GRAY SERGE SKIRT, A MATCHING DARK GRAY WOOL FUR-TRIMMED JACKET OVER A CRISP WHITE BLOUSE, LOW-HEELED SHOES, DOESKIN GLOVES, A LEATHER PURSE ATTACHED TO A BICYCLE BELT, AND A WHITE HELMET. AND NOW, OUTFITTED IN BICYCLE FINERY, SHE IS OFF!

Lessons in Bicycle Riding

BUY ONE OF THE OLD-FASHIONED TO BEGIN UPON; THESE MAY BE GOT AT A REASONABLE PRICE, AS MANY HAVE BEEN DISCARDED FOR THE MODERN ONES. THEY ARE CALLED "PRACTICERS," OR, MORE FAMILIARLY, "BONE-SHAKERS." IN LEARNING TO RIDE, IT IS ADVISABLE TO HAVE A COMPETENT TEACHER, WHO CANNOT ONLY SHOW WHAT IS WANTED, BUT CAN ALSO PUT THE BEGINNER IN THE WAY OF DOING IT HIMSELF.... OF COURSE IT IS NECESSARY TO HAVE RECOURSE TO A FRIENDLY ARM, AND THERE MAY BE MANY CASES IN WHICH TWO FRIENDS ARE DESIROUS TO LEARN THE BICYCLE, AND CAN GIVE MUTUAL HELP.

—COLLIER'S CYCLOPEDIA OF SOCIAL AND COMMERCIAL INFORMATION

Inclement weather cannot prevent the Victorian lady from finding pleasure in her hobbies, for she is a woman creative and resourceful, and she finds ever so many ways to pass the time indoors. She may arrange her collections of wildflowers, seashells, or butterflies into artistic displays in her parlor, or take up a new interest—watercolor or oil painting, pressing flowers, copying pencil drawings, painting fire screens, putting together scrapbooks and albums of photographs. During quiet evenings at home she and her family enjoy billiards, chess, cards, backgammon, memory and skill games, and kaleidoscopes.

Alone in her special corner of the house, she loses herself in the pages of current novels—Austen, Dickens, Eliot—and her favorite poets, perhaps Scott, Byron, and Tennyson. She also may enjoy the plays of Shakespeare and the romance of books like *Arabian Nights*. And she might begin or end each day by writing in her journal, reflecting upon the people and events that have made that day like no other.

I think I have never told you that
I am reading Vanity Fair *and think it delicious.*
—LADY EMILY LUTYENS, *A BLESSED GIRL*

Entertaining Parlor Games

✿ CONSEQUENCES:

THIS IS A CAPITAL INDOOR TABLE GAME, ESPECIALLY WHEN THERE ARE SOME TEN OR A DOZEN PLAYERS TO KEEP THE GAME ALIVE. IT IS FOUNDED UPON THE ABSURD INCONGRUITIES THAT RESULT WHEN A NUMBER OF PEOPLE COMBINE TOGETHER TO MAKE ONE CONNECTED SENTENCE, EACH TAKING HIS OWN PART IRRESPECTIVE OF EACH AND ALL OF THE OTHERS.

✿ ADJECTIVES:

THIS IS ALSO A VERY AMUSING GAME. ONE OF THE PLAYERS WRITES A LETTER, WHICH OF COURSE HE DOES NOT SHOW, LEAVING A BLANK FOR EVERY ADJECTIVE. HE THEN ASKS EACH PLAYER IN TURN ROUND THE TABLE FOR AN ADJECTIVE, FILLING UP THE BLANK SPACES WITH THE ADJECTIVES AS HE RECEIVES THEM.

✿ DEFINITIONS:

THE THEORY OF THIS GAME IS VERY SIMPLE, BUT THE OPENING IT GIVES FOR WIT AND SATIRE IS SIMPLY UNBOUNDED, AND FOR PURE INTELLECTUALITY IT STANDS UNRIVALED AMONGST EVENING GAMES. THE PLAYERS SIT ROUND A TABLE EACH WITH A PENCIL AND PIECE OF PAPER; A NOUN IS THEN SELECTED AT RANDOM FROM A LIST, OR IN ANY CONVENIENT WAY, AND EACH IS THEN BOUND TO FURNISH AN ORIGINAL DEFINITION. THIS DONE, ANOTHER IS GIVEN OUT AND SIMILARLY DEFINED. WHEN A CONVENIENT NUMBER HAVE BEEN THUS DISPOSED OF, THE PAPERS ARE HANDED UP TO THE PRESIDENT, WHO IS CHOSEN FOR THE OCCASION, AND THE SEVERAL DEFINITIONS READ ALOUD. SOME VERY BRILLIANT IMPROMPTUS ARE SOMETIMES FLUNG OFF IN THIS MANNER; AND WE WOULD STRONGLY ADVISE, WHERE THE GAME IS MUCH PLAYED, THAT A BOOK SHOULD BE KEPT FOR THE ENSHRINEMENT OF THE SPECIAL FLOWERS OF WIT.

❀ Forfeits:

When a player has to pay a forfeit, he gives in pledge some piece of portable property, which he will afterwards, at the end of the game, have to redeem in due order. One player is declared judge, and, with eyes blindfolded stands with his face to the wall, while another takes up the several pledges separately and asks, "Here is a pretty thing, and a very pretty thing; what is to be done to the owner of this very pretty thing?" Or, omitting the formula, asks merely, "What is to be done to the owner of this?" The blindfolded player, who, of course, does not know to whom each forfeit belongs, and therefore cannot be accused of unfairness, assigns for each forfeit a task which must be fulfilled before the pledge can be reclaimed.

—*Collier's Cyclopedia of Social and Commercial Information (1882)*

❀ Head, Body, Legs

This is an easy paper game, and popular, especially with the younger members of the party. To each player is given a strip of paper, on which he draws a head of some sort, without telling or showing any one the kind of head he has drawn. He then folds the paper in such a way that nothing but the two lines of the neck are visible. The paper is then passed on to his neighbour, who attaches to the neck some sort of body. The paper is again folded, leaving only the lines for the beginning of the legs, and passed on to the next person, who has to add the legs, though he has no idea what the body is like. The completed drawing is passed on again and then opened, and sent round for all to see. The completed animals are usually very funny.

—*How to Entertain Your Guests*

Her society champions an alert, well-educated mind, and the Victorian lady obliges by reading about interesting new subjects and visiting lecture halls. Perhaps she spends her morning immersed in language studies—French or German, Italian or Russian—and scours the latest volumes on painting or architecture before afternoon tea. Or she might travel with friends to a lecture hall and listen to presentations on astronomy, science, economics, art, or geography. If the chosen topic is philosophy, she may supplement her lecture notes with readings from Plato, Aristotle, Kant, or Mill.

Music holds a special place in her heart, and she adores singing, playing, and dancing. If she is musically talented, she could be proficient on two or more instruments, piano, harp, and flute, or violin and cello. She is enraptured by the great works of Handel, Bach, Mendelssohn, and Beethoven. Concerts, operas, and private musical evenings make up a good part of her social activities. Hers is, in every way, a "well-rounded" education. Conversing with her will surely be a delight.

In addition to improving herself, the Victorian lady seeks to better the lives of others. She can often be found out in her village, performing charitable deeds for the poor and the sick. She might take part in the annual church bazaar to raise money for worthy causes, such as hospitals and orphanages, or perhaps she lends a welcome hand in the village schoolhouse. She is a compassionate lady of varied interests and talents, full of life and the joy of living it each and every day.

Good books, like good friends,
are few and chosen; the more select,
the more enjoyable.

—LOUISA MAY ALCOTT

She speaks and writes perfectly well English, French, German, Italian, & of course, the Russian language. She understands chemistry, mathematics & botany, draws, paints, plays on the piano & dances & embroiders very well. Her knowledge of general literature & history is extensive, & her conversation animated and amusing. She has a deep feeling & just knowledge of the fine arts. The learned men call her un miracle.

—HARRIET GARNETT, WRITING OF A CHARMING AND TALENTED ACQUAINTANCE

Chapter Four
A DELIGHTFUL ROMANCE

Who can find a virtuous woman? For her price is far above rubies.

—THE BOOK OF PROVERBS

A chance meeting at the village Christmas ball. Love letters penned by a devoted suitor in the springtime, their delivery anxiously awaited by the fair lady. A well-mannered courtship, the much-hoped-for proposal, a grand wedding followed by a honeymoon tour of Europe or, perhaps,

Breathless, we flung us on the windy hill,
Laughed in the sun, and kissed the lovely grass.

—RUPERT BROOKE

Gentlemen begin to court the Victorian lady when she is fourteen or fifteen, where the veil of girlhood is lifted to reveal a delightful young woman.

a month spent just with each other at a countryside cottage. And, after all the pomp and grandeur, when she arrives at her new home, the Victorian lady discovers the true happiness of lifelong companionship—the shared private smiles, steadfast mutual support, and deepening bond of the ideal love match.

She might meet a special young man at an ice skating party, catch a glimpse of him at her "coming out" ball, or entertain his earnest attentions at a country dance. Perhaps she finds herself playing piano at a musical party when a young gentleman steps forward to accompany her with his excellent voice. At one of the many dances she attends, her future mate's name could be scribbled among those on her dance card. When he begins to court her, after first seeking her permission as well as the approval of her parents, they will politely refer to each other as "Mister" and "Miss." And he will bring the young lady only the most proper of calling gifts—flowers, candy, a favorite book.

Rosy is the West,
Rosy is the South,
Rosy are her cheeks,
And a rose her mouth.

—ALFRED, LORD TENNYSON, "MAUD"

Her face blushed with rosy health, and her lips with the freshest of smiles, and she had a pair of eyes which sparkled with the brightest and honestest of good-humour.

—WILLIAM MAKEPEACE THACKERAY

Light was her slender nose
Tip-tilted like the petal of a flower.

—ALFRED, LORD TENNYSON

A Proper Letter from a Gentleman, Asking Her Permission to Pay His Addresses

18 W. 36TH ST., N.Y.,
JULY 27, 1882

DEAR MISS WINSLOW:

I must crave your pardon for the somewhat bold address I am about to make, trusting that its apparent presumption may be excused by the consideration that my feelings are deeply enlisted in its success. The marked attentions paid to you at Mrs. Burke's party could not, I flatter myself, have failed to attract your notice, nor have been wholly disagreeable to yourself. Cherishing this pleasing belief, I am encouraged to crave the privilege of being permitted to improve my acquaintance with a lady for whom I entertain so high an esteem.

The company in which we met will, I trust, be considered a sufficient guarantee of my character and position to warrant me in looking forward to an early renewal of the happy hours spent in your company. Your kind permission once granted, I shall lose no time in seeking, for my addresses, the sanction of your parents; but I do not feel at liberty to take such a step until well assured that it will be agreeable to your wishes.

May I entreat the favor of an early reply? which, dear Miss Winslow, will be anxiously awaited by

YOUR DEVOTED ADMIRER,

WILLIAM THROPCAKE

—COLLIER'S CYCLOPEDIA OF SOCIAL AND COMMERCIAL INFORMATION

Tokens of Love— A Damask Rose

IF A LOVER PRESENTS
A FULL-BLOWN DAMASK
ROSE TO HIS LADY-LOVE,
HE IS ABOUT TO OFFER
HER HIS HEART AND HAND
IN MARRIAGE:

"THE DAMASK ROSE,
GIVEN *in* FULL BLOOM,

GIVES UNTO COURTSHIP'S
DAYS *their* DOOM;

IT HERALDS *the* HAPPY
DAY *of* DAYS,

WHEN HEARTS UNITE *in*
WEDLOCK'S WAYS."

—*A Garter Round the Bedpost*

The next step of a favorable courtship is, quite naturally, the engagement. A young lady's marriage proposal could happen during the magical evening hours in a hidden corner of the ballroom. Or perhaps her suitor will arrive at her home in the morning hours, rushing her into the parlor and declaring his love for her while on his knees, which is, of course, the suitable posture adopted by a young man asking this most important of questions. Proposal accepted, the happy couple exchanges rings—fashioned of heavy gold and adorned with pearls, diamonds, rubies, sapphires, amethysts, or other precious stones—and announces their happiness to the village or town.

To be accepted by you as your husband and the earthly guardian of your welfare I should regard as the highest of providential gifts.

—GEORGE ELIOT

The Qualities of a Lover

THE REQUISITES MOST ESSENTIAL IN A LOVER ARE:

❀ AN AGREEABLE PERSON.

❀ ACCOMPLISHED MANNERS.

❀ SWEETNESS *of* TEMPER *and* DISPOSITION.

❀ FREE FROM LEVITY *and* ANYTHING BORDERING *on the* RIDICULOUS.

❀ AN UNBLEMISHED REPUTATION.

❀ A MIND STORED *with* VIRTUOUS PRINCIPLES.

WITH A PARTNER OF THIS KIND, NONE NEED FEAR TO VENTURE UPON THE STREAM OF MATRIMONY.

—THE ETIQUETTE OF LOVE AND COURTSHIP

And then comes that fairy tale moment that plays on the stage of every young girl's dreams—the wedding, that blessed event where two hearts indeed become one. The bride, "fair as is the rose in May" and dressed in white, cream, or often a gown in a watercolor hue of lavender, pale peach, or apple blossom green, carries a bouquet of orange blossoms with her hair done up in a coronet of roses. The house, gardens, or church are dressed for the event in their finest blossoms and greenery, and music from a majestic organ or deep cello sings out the wonder of love. The guests will present the happy pair with well-chosen and useful gifts—fine china, teapots, poetry books, and paintings.

But it was a happy and beautiful bride who came down the old, homespun-carpeted stairs that September noon—the first bride of Green Gables, slender and shining-eyed, in the mist of her maiden veil, with her arms full of roses. Gilbert, waiting for her in the hall below, looked up at her with adoring eyes. She was his at last, this evasive, long-sought Anne, won after years of patient waiting.

—LUCY MAUD MONTGOMERY, ANNE'S HOUSE OF DREAMS

Love is patient, love is kind...It always protects, always trusts, always hopes, always perseveres. Love never fails.

—THE BOOK OF I CORINTHIANS

And after the vows are said with eyes starry and voices soft but true, the new husband and wife will be swept away in a horse-drawn carriage to their honeymoon journey—a tour of Italy, France, and Switzerland, a fortnight at a seaside resort, or a journey to an undisclosed but enchanting location.

The Victorian lady has promised to love and cherish her husband, and he has promised her the same. She is his confidante, his primary advisor, his chosen partner in life. They are lovers and friends, the best of companions, each thinking first of the other. Kindred spirits to explore their world hand in hand.

How do I love thee? Let me count the ways.
I love thee to the depth and breadth and height
My soul can reach, when feeling out of sight.
For the ends of being and ideal Grace.
I love thee to the level of everyday's
Most quiet need, by sun and candlelight.

—Elizabeth Barrett Browning

Never meet your husband without a smile.

—Happy Homes and How to Make Them

My heart is like a singing bird
Whose nest is in a watered shoot;
My heart is like an apple-tree
Whose boughs are bent with thickset fruit;
My heart is like a rainbow shell
That paddles in a halcyon sea;
My heart is gladder than all these
Because my love is come to me.

—Christina Rossetti, "A Birthday"

Chapter Five
THE WONDER OF MOTHERHOOD

*Happy he
With such a mother! faith in womankind
Beats with his blood, and trust in all things high
Comes easy to him...*
—ALFRED, LORD TENNYSON

From the moment she births them into the world, the Victorian mother teaches and guides, encourages and loves her small charges. Drawing on her rich heritage of faith, knowledge, and love, and using her home and the splendid outdoors as the children's first classroom, she embraces the happy task of motherhood with patience, caring, and a spirit of joy.

*Mother's arms under you,
Her eyes above you
Sing it high, sing it low,
Love me,—I love you.*
—CHRISTINA ROSSETTI

*By the fireside, still the light is shining,
The children's arms round the parents twining.*
—D.M. MULOCK

Very young boys and girls learn their first simple prayers and soothing lullabies from Mother. With her, they explore the miracles of nature—leaping green grasshoppers, sunflowers that seemingly become giants overnight—and thus begin their study of the amazing world. The Victorian lady teaches her small daughters the domestic arts—baking and mending, as well as creating their own signature beauty in the home. The handiwork she learned from her own mother—samplers, embroidery, needlework—she will pass down to the next generation. Young sons learn equally important lessons—how to light the hearth, the right method for saddling up a horse, the proper way to address a lady. When the children are a bit older, Mother will set them upon their first courses of study. Lessons might include language studies of French, Latin, and Greek, geography and arithmetic, writing and spelling, dancing and exercise. And, of course, she gives her children daily guidance in developing a strong, fine character.

"The time has come," the Walrus said,
"To talk of many things:
Of shoes—and ships—and sealing wax—
Of cabbages—and kings—"

—LEWIS CARROLL, *THROUGH THE LOOKING GLASS*

Train up a child in the way he should go:
and when he is old, he will not depart from it.

—THE BOOK OF PROVERBS

And no childhood would be quite complete without a good supply of toys, games, and books to lead little ones on make-believe journeys. The Victorian lady chooses suitable toys for each of her children—dolls and dollhouses, play sewing machines and wooden horses, fire engines and trains.

A Child's Virtues

A GOOD PART OF A VICTORIAN CHILD'S EDUCATION IS THE LEARNING AND PRACTICE OF INDISPENSABLE VIRTUES, WHICH ARE BOTH TAUGHT AND MODELED BY MOTHER. A LIST OF VIRTUES ALMOST ALWAYS INCLUDES THE FOLLOWING—

- PIETY
- INTEGRITY
- FORTITUDE
- CHARITY
- OBEDIENCE
- CONSIDERATION
- SINCERITY
- PRUDENCE
- ACTIVITY
- CHEERFULNESS

—THE YOUNG LADY'S BOOK

Games for Children

🦋 BUTTERFLIES

THREE SMALL POTS OF PAINT, OF DIFFERENT COLORS, (E.G. RED, YELLOW AND BLUE), AND A SMALL BRUSH MUST BE PROCURED BEFORE-HAND. EACH PLAYER TAKES A CLEAN SHEET OF NOTEPAPER, AND, HAVING WRITTEN HIS NAME ON THE BACK, PUTS TWO DOTS OF PAINT, CHOOSING WHICH TWO OF THE THREE COLORS HE LIKES, ONE JUST ABOVE THE OTHER IN THE MIDDLE OF THE SHEET. THIS HE DOUBLES DOWN THE MIDDLE AND PRESSES OUTWARDS, WITH A FLAT KNIFE, IN THE SHAPE OF A BUTTERFLY'S WINGS. THE PAPER IS THEN OPENED, AND WITH A PEN INK FEELERS ARE ADDED. THE BEST BUTTERFLY WINS THE PRIZE.

🎈 BALLOONS

THIS IS A GAME IN WHICH THE PLAYERS ARE DIVIDED INTO TWO SIDES, AND SEATED IN TWO STRAIGHT ROWS, FOUR OR FIVE FEET APART. AT AN EQUAL DISTANCE BETWEEN THE CHAIRS, A TAPE OR STRING IS TIGHTLY FIXED ON THE FLOOR. A TOY BAL-LOON IS THEN THROWN UP INTO THE AIR, EACH SIDE TRYING TO GET THE BALLOON ON TO THE FLOOR ON THE OTHER SIDE OF THE TAPE. SHOULD IT FALL ON THEIR OWN SIDE OF THE TAPE, ONE GOAL IS COUNTED TO THEIR OPPONENTS, BUT IF ON THE OTHER, THEY SCORE THE GOAL. THE PLAYERS MUST REMAIN SEATED, AND HIT THE BALLOON WITH THE BACK OF

THE RIGHT HAND ONLY. THE SIDE AGAINST WHOM THE GOAL IS SCORED HAS THE PRIVILEGE OF "KICKING OFF," I.E. THROWING UP THE BALLOON TO START AGAIN. THE GAME CONTINUES UNTIL ONE SIDE HAS SCORED THIRTEEN GOALS (OR ANY NUMBER THAT HAS BEEN DECIDED ON BEFOREHAND). IT IS ADVISABLE TO HAVE TWO OR THREE BALLOONS IN RESERVE!

FAMILY COACH

THIS IS AN EVER-POPULAR GAME WITH SCHOOL-CHILDREN, BOYS AND GIRLS. THE PLAYERS MUST SIT ROUND THE ROOM AND EACH CHOOSE SOME PART OF THE FAMILY COACH—THE WHEEL, THE AXLE, THE WHIP, THE SEAT, MRS. BROWN, HER BABY, THE CAT, ETC., ETC. ONE OF THE GROWN-UPS MUST THEN TELL THE TALE OF MRS. BROWN'S JOURNEY IN THE COACH, AND OF THE ACCIDENTS THAT BEFELL THEM; HOW ONE OF THE WHEELS CAME OFF, THE AXLE BROKE, THE BABY CRIED AND SO ON, MAKING IT UP AS SHE GOES ALONG. AT THE MENTION OF EACH SPECIFIC PART, THE MEMBER WHO HAS CHOSEN THAT PART MUST STAND UP AND TURN ROUND. BUT SHOULD THE WORDS "FAMILY COACH" BE MENTIONED, ALL THE PLAYERS MUST CHANGE THEIR SEATS. SHOULD ANY FAIL TO DO THIS, OR TO ANSWER HIS CUE WHEN HIS PART OF THE COACH IS MENTIONED, HE MUST PAY A FORFEIT.

—HOW TO ENTERTAIN YOUR GUESTS

Younger ones delight in the blocks, music boxes, rocking horses, woolly animals, and Noah's ark, while older children bring out the jigsaw puzzles, maps, kites, hoops, and tops for hours upon hours of merriment.

A smell of crushed grass hangs over the unmown lawn, where the lush new blades lie trodden in all directions by children's games.

—COLETTE, *MY MOTHER'S HOUSE*

Card games, anagrams, and riddles work just as well for amusement as they do for learning. And then there are the books—picture books, story books, scrapbooks, books of paper dolls, poetry books, and books of fairy tales. Oh, the delightful books! As children drift off to the Land of Nod, Mother's gentle voice reads from "Swiss Family Robinson," "Andersen's Fairy Tales," or perhaps from a collection of inspiring Bible stories.

I am at tea in my nursery and rather bored. Suddenly my mother comes in, and everything is bright and cheerful again. She is in a blue and white striped dress with full sleeves...and she has brought some tiny cakes. Some have five pointed crowns with angelica on them. Others are like bunches of filberts.... When the table is cleared my mother cuts out a row of little paper ladies in crinolines and with joined hands. She blows, and they glide across the table to me as if moved by magic.

—F. ANSTEY

What girl is more popular, not only among the little ones, but also with "children of the larger growth," than she who "knows many games," and can keep the youngsters interested and amused, while the knowledge of her power makes her enjoy the sport herself.

—THE YOUNG LADIES' TREASURE BOOK

As her small ones spread their wings to climb high in an apple tree, spend a first weekend away from home at a friend's country manor, or set off down the garden path to discover, all alone, a secret corner of the world, a mother smiles as she watches them go, arms outstretched, ready to enfold them with love and acceptance on their return, ready to lend a listening ear to adventures and observations. After all, a not-so-small part of her journeys with them.

In winter I get up at night
And dress by yellow candle-light.
In summer, quite the other way,—
I have to go to bed by day.
I have to go to bed and see
The birds still hopping on the tree,
Or hear the grown-up people's feet
Still going past me in the street.

—ROBERT LOUIS STEVENSON, "BED IN SUMMER"

Almighty God, heavenly Father, you have blessed us with the joy and care of children: Give us calm strength and patient wisdom as we bring them up, that we may teach them to love whatever is just and true and good, following the example of our Savior Jesus Christ. Amen.

—*THE BOOK OF COMMON PRAYER*

Letters from Children

THE VICTORIAN MOTHER UNFAILINGLY TEACHES HER CHILDREN THE ART OF CORRESPONDENCE. HERE THE DAUGHTER, MARY, PRACTICES LETTER-WRITING BY COMPOSING A SHORT LETTER INTRODUCING A SISTER TO A SCHOOLMATE.

Wilkesbarre, June 8, 1882
Dear Rosie:
This letter will introduce my sister Polly.
I do not think that I need say another
word. I love you both. You will love both of
us. I will write a long letter very soon.

Yours, as Ever,
Mary.

—COLLIER'S CYCLOPEDIA OF SOCIAL AND COMMERCIAL INFORMATION

Chapter Six
THE ART OF ENTERTAINING

The house had been arranged that it was impossible to know where you were,
when once in it. The hall was a paradise. The staircase was fairyland.
The lobbies were grottoes rich with ferns.

—ANTHONY TROLLOPE

Tis the season for balls and tea parties, musical evenings and house parties. Tis the season for paying and receiving calls, for hosting and attending breakfast and dinner parties. Summer or winter, spring or autumn, it is always the season for entertaining in the Victorian lady's life!

The Victorian lady's everyday social obligations consist primarily of paying and receiving calls. She traditionally pays a formal call to the hostess following a dinner or ball, and always calls on her new neighbors. She makes her calls at a specific time of day, morning or afternoon, and makes sure to leave her calling card if the lady of the house is not at home. Generally her visits last no longer than fifteen minutes, and both parties usually keep the conversation to polite small talk.

She has the opportunity to spend more time with her friends and neighbors when she puts on or attends breakfast parties, luncheons, five o'clock teas, or afternoon "At Home" parties, of which the most popular attractions are professional or amateur musicians and plenty of refreshments. From the time she was a young girl hosting tea parties for her dolls and play animals, the Victorian lady has acquired admirable conversation skills and practiced the rules of etiquette that enable her to be a most delightful hostess—and a beloved guest!

Quite half of the acquirements of a good social talker depend on being a good listener also.
—THE YOUNG LADIES' TREASURE BOOK

A word fitly spoken is like apples of gold in pictures of silver.
—THE BOOK OF PROVERBS

And then there are the very formal occasions—the enchanting balls, the "coming out" parties, the dinner and evening parties, the grand house parties held in country manors. These are the occasions when the entire house and garden are transformed into a fairyland, where the finest dresses and the best china and the most inspired desserts transform the evening.

And each type of party boasts its own special attraction. Guests look forward to emotional performances at the musical evening parties, seeking out talented performers from the audience at hand, thrilled to discover a brilliant soloist or an accomplished pianist among their peers. Everlasting fun rules at the weekend house parties in the country, where

The Etiquette of Paying Calls

❀ VISITS OF CEREMONY SHOULD BE SHORT. IF EVEN THE CONVERSATION SHOULD HAVE BECOME ANIMATED, BEWARE OF LETTING YOUR CALL EXCEED HALF-AN-HOUR'S LENGTH. IT IS ALWAYS BETTER TO LET YOUR FRIENDS REGRET RATHER THAN DESIRE YOUR WITHDRAWAL.

❀ SHOULD THERE BE DAUGHTERS OR SISTERS RESIDING WITH THE LADY UPON WHOM YOU CALL, YOU MAY TURN DOWN A CORNER OF YOUR CARD TO SIGNIFY THAT THE VISIT IS PAID TO ALL. IT IS IN BETTER TASTE, HOWEVER, TO LEAVE CARDS FOR EACH.

❀ NEVER TAKE A FAVORITE DOG INTO A DRAWING-ROOM WHEN YOU MAKE A MORNING CALL. THEIR FEET MAY BE DUSTY, OR THEY MAY BARK AT THE SIGHT OF STRANGERS, OR, BEING OF A TOO FRIENDLY DISPOSITION, MAY TAKE THE LIBERTY OF LYING ON A LADY'S GOWN, OR JUMPING ON THE SOFAS AND EASY CHAIRS.

—COLLIER'S CYCLOPEDIA OF SOCIAL AND COMMERCIAL INFORMATION

A Proper Introduction

❀ WHEN INTRODUCED TO A GEN-
TLEMAN, NEVER OFFER YOUR HAND.
WHEN INTRODUCED, PERSONS LIMIT
THEIR RECOGNITION OF EACH OTHER
TO A BOW.

❀ IF YOU ARE WALKING WITH ONE
FRIEND, AND PRESENTLY MEET WITH,
OR ARE JOINED BY, A SECOND, DO
NOT COMMIT THE TOO FREQUENT
ERROR OF INTRODUCING THEM TO
EACH OTHER. YOU HAVE EVEN LESS
RIGHT TO DO SO THAN IF THEY
ENCOUNTERED EACH OTHER AT YOUR
HOUSE DURING A MORNING CALL.

❀ PERSONS WHO HAVE MET AT THE
HOUSE OF A MUTUAL FRIEND WITH-
OUT BEING INTRODUCED SHOULD
NOT BOW IF THEY AFTERWARDS
MEET ELSEWHERE. A BOW IMPLIES
ACQUAINTANCE; AND PERSONS WHO
HAVE NOT BEEN INTRODUCED ARE
NOT ACQUAINTED.

—COLLIER'S CYCLOPEDIA OF SOCIAL AND
COMMERCIAL INFORMATION

energetic guests play games and take part in charades and dramatic presentations, and gentlemen spin ladies round on the dance floor every evening, with the band playing waltzes, polkas, square dances, and reels. Fortunate children attend their own special balls given by the Queen, and formal balls for the grown-ups feature string quartets playing the music of Mozart, Haydn, Beethoven, and Bach. Grand occasions these are, occasions for laughter and celebration, good friends and good cheer.

However small and simple the music-room may be,
it should always appear as though there were space
overhead for the notes to escape.

—EDITH WHARTON

As we crossed the great hall on the way to our rooms I realised for the first time
how the house lent itself to the occasion, and how beautiful the rooms were look-
ing. Even the drawing-room, formal and cold to my consideration when we were
alone, was a blaze of colour now, flowers in every corner, red roses in silver bowls
on the white cloth of the supper table, the long windows open to the terrace,
where, as soon as it was dusk, the fairy lights would shine.

—DAPHNE DU MAURIER, REBECCA

THE PROPER INVITATION

Mr. and Mrs. Henry A. Bogert
At Home
Saturday, November 5th, from
3 to 6 o'clock P.M.
Flushing

Mrs. Molyneux requests the honor
of Captain Hamilton's company
at an evening party, on Monday,
March the 11th instant.
Dancing will begin at Nine o'clock.
Thursday, March 1st.

Mrs. E.S. Phydes
requests the pleasure of your company
Monday evening, February twelfth,
at eight o'clock
Masquerade
155 East 36th St.,
R.S.V.P.

—Collier's Cyclopedia of Social and Commercial Information

Some Situations You Might Encounter at Morning or Evening Parties, or at Balls

❀ IF YOU ARE AT THE HOUSE OF A NEW ACQUAINTANCE AND FIND YOURSELF AMONG ENTIRE STRANGERS, REMEMBER THAT BY SO MEETING UNDER ONE ROOF YOU ARE ALL IN A CERTAIN SENSE MADE KNOWN TO ONE ANOTHER, AND SHOULD, THEREFORE, CONVERSE FREELY, AS EQUALS. TO SHRINK AWAY TO A SIDE-TABLE AND AFFECT TO BE ABSORBED IN SOME ALBUM OR ILLUSTRATED WORK; OR, IF YOU FIND ONE UNLUCKY ACQUAINTANCE IN THE ROOM TO FASTEN UPON HER LIKE A DROWNING MAN CLINGING TO A SPAR, ARE *GAUCHERIES* WHICH NO SHYNESS CAN EXCUSE.

❀ IF YOU POSSESS ANY MUSICAL ACCOMPLISHMENTS, DO NOT WAIT TO BE PRESSED AND ENTREATED BY YOUR HOSTESS, BUT COMPLY IMMEDIATELY WHEN SHE PAYS YOU THE COMPLIMENT OF INVITING YOU TO PLAY OR SING. REMEMBER, HOWEVER, THAT ONLY THE LADY OF THE HOUSE HAS THE RIGHT TO ASK YOU. IF OTHERS DO SO, YOU CAN PUT THEM OFF IN SOME POLITE WAY, BUT MUST NOT COMPLY TILL THE HOSTESS HERSELF INVITES YOU.

❀ IMPROMPTU CHARADES ARE FREQUENTLY ORGANIZED AT FRIENDLY PARTIES. UNLESS YOU HAVE REALLY SOME TALENT FOR ACTING AND SOME READINESS OF SPEECH, YOU SHOULD REMEMBER THAT YOU ONLY PUT OTHERS OUT AND EXPOSE YOUR OWN INABILITY BY TAKING PART IN THESE ENTERTAINMENTS. OF COURSE, IF YOUR HELP IS REALLY NEEDED, AND YOU WOULD DISOBLIGE BY REFUSING, YOU MUST DO YOUR BEST, AND BY DOING IT AS QUIETLY AND COOLLY AS POSSIBLE, AVOID BEING AWKWARD OR RIDICULOUS.

—Collier's Cyclopedia of Social and Commercial Information

Chapter Seven
SIT DOWN AND DINE WITH ME

Stands the Church clock at ten to three?
And is there honey still for tea?

—RUPERT BROOKE

The day begins with the impressive parade of breakfast delicacies, then marches on to a light mid-morning repast and perhaps a leisurely luncheon. As the sun lowers in the sky, the tea scones and sandwiches are prepared and the tea table dressed in its white linen best, followed several hours later by the grand finalé—the dinner presentation, in its formal abundance.

Polly put the kettle on, we'll all have tea.

—CHARLES DICKENS, *BARNABY RUDGE*

Life, within doors, has few pleasanter prospects than a neatly arranged and well-provisioned breakfast table.

—NATHANIEL HAWTHORNE, *THE HOUSE OF SEVEN GABLES*

The Victorian lady considers breakfast a most important meal in her day, and she fills her plate with the wide variety of delicacies heaped on the sideboard—bacon and eggs; ham, beef, and fish; muffins, crumpets, and other assorted breads; tea, coffee, and even a bit of chocolate. In some households a mid-morning meal, consisting of cake, biscuits, and light beverages, is served. Luncheon is a good time for the lady to gather together with friends, sharing conversation and exchanging a bit of gossip over seasonal soups and salads. And then there is dinner—generally served at six, the much-anticipated social event of the day. Country or city, cottage or mansion, everyone dresses for the dinner.

Why, sometimes I've believed
as many as six impossible things before breakfast.

—LEWIS CARROLL, *THROUGH THE LOOKING GLASS*

How impressed I was . . . by the magnificence of the breakfast
offered to us. There was tea, in a great silver urn, and coffee too,
and on the heater, piping hot, dishes of scrambled eggs, of bacon, and
another of fish. There was a little clutch of boiled eggs as well, and in their
own special heater, and porridge, in a silver porringer. On another side-board
was a ham, and a great piece of cold bacon. There were scones too,
on the table, and toast, and various plots of jam, marmalade, and honey,
while dessert dishes, piled high with fruit, stood at either end.

—DAPHNE DE MAURIER, *REBECCA*

The Victorian dinners, in particular, are quite well known for endless processions of soups and meats, salads and puddings, ices and meringues. A dinner at a country manor weekend party, for instance, consists of at least nine courses, with plenty of time allowed between each course to permit each guest to fully enjoy the variety of courses.

Menu for a Dinner Party

CLEAR SOUP, TURTLE SOUP, COLD VICHYSSOISE

CHEESE AND GRAPES

BRANDY CHERRIES, CAKES AND BUNS

SALMON IN SAUCE, LOBSTER SALAD, BOILED TURBOT

OYSTER PATTIES, HEAVY SALAD, ROASTED POTATOES

ROAST MUTTON, LAMB CUTLETS, COLD VEGETABLES

DUCK, PHEASANT, TURKEY, WOODCOCK, PLUM PUDDING

ASPIC, BOILED FOWL AND TONGUE, CURRANT JELLY

MERINGUES, CHOCOLATES, MARASCHINO JELLY

FANTASTICAL ICE CREAM CASTLES AND FLOWERS

CHAMPAGNE TRUFFLES, ICES AND SORBETS

COFFEE AND TEA, STRAWBERRIES IN SEASON

A Proper Tea

PUTTING ON A PROPER VICTORIAN TEA IS NO EASY TASK. YOU MUST START YOUR PLANNING WEEKS— MONTHS, EVEN—IN ADVANCE, DRAWING UP THE GUEST LIST, SENDING OUT INVITATIONS ON THE NICEST OF PAPERS, PREPARING YOUR DECORATIONS, AND, OF COURSE, CREATING A FIRST-RATE TEA TABLE! TO MAKE CERTAIN NO DETAIL IS LEFT UNATTENDED, IT IS HELPFUL TO PEN A LIST OF TEA PARTY ESSENTIALS—

A MIX *of* CHARMING GUESTS SURE *to* ENJOY EACH OTHER'S COMPANY

YOUR BEST SILVER TEA SET, *and* BRIGHTLY POLISHED SILVERWARE

SPOTLESS LINEN *or* LACE TABLE CLOTHS *and* SERVIETTES

THE FINEST FLOWERS *from* YOUR GARDEN—ROSES *and* QUEEN ANNE'S LACE, DELPHINIUM *and* PHLOX

SOOTHING MUSIC— BACH'S *BRANDENBURG CONCERTOS*, PERHAPS

COLD LEMONADE *on a* WARM SUMMER DAY

CREAM *and* SUGAR *for the* PERFECTLY BREWED TEA

A VARIETY *of* DAINTY SANDWICHES—WATERCRESS, CHICKEN SALAD, ETC., ETC.

SCONES, MUFFINS, BISCUITS, BUNS, *and* SHORTBREAD

FRESH STRAWBERRIES, PEACHES, *and* OTHER SEASONAL FRUIT

TEACAKES *and* PETITS FOURS

In addition to a sit-down dinner, the hostess of a ball makes preparations for a running buffet table laden with cold roast chicken and beef, meat pies, salmon or lobster, a variety of sandwiches, and a tray filled with rich desserts.

Besides the food itself, the dining table requires the finest settings of china, crystal, and silver, topped off by a decorative centerpiece. A cornucopia filled with the bounty of harvest suffices well for a simple breakfast or luncheon, and flowers are standard for the tea table, but the event of dinner calls for grand arrangements of plants and flowers, an ice sculpture, or perhaps a fantastical ice cream castle.

> *I said when we were sitting down to dinner on Sunday evening that I hailed the arrival of evening because it was (socially) the pick of the day, to which Con replied, in her delicious way, that she liked breakfast here from the thought that she now had a whole day before her, and lunch because there was still half the day to come, and dinner because she did not care that so much of the day was gone since the prime of it remained. Did anybody ever express a delightful idea more delightfully?*
>
> —LADY EMILY LUTYENS, *A BLESSED GIRL*

As a general rule, mealtime conversation is kept light and entertaining—the latest ideas in science or politics (no heated debate, if you please!), witticisms and literature, farming and agriculture, personal tidbits or, of course, favorable comments about the endless procession of tasty dishes are always quite welcome. A good Victorian hostess does her best to make sure that everything is pleasing to her guests—the food, the company, and the conversation. *Bon appétit*!

*I think of half-past four at Manderley,
and the table drawn before the library fire. The door
flung open, punctual to the minute, and the
performance, never-varying, of the laying of the tea, the
silver tray, the kettle, the snowy cloth....Those dripping
crumpets, I can see them now. Tiny crisp wedges of
toast, the piping-hot, flaky scones. Sandwiches of
unknown nature, mysteriously flavoured and quite
delectable, and that very special gingerbread.*

—DAPHNE DU MAURIER, *REBECCA*

*"I can just imagine myself sitting down
at the head of the table and pouring out the tea,"
said Anne, shutting her eyes ecstatically. "And asking
Diana if she takes sugar! I know she doesn't but of
course I'll ask her just as if I didn't know. And then
pressing her to take another piece of fruit-cake
and another helping of preserves...."*

—L.M. MONTGOMERY, *ANNE OF GREEN GABLES*

*Blessed are you, O Lord God, King of the Universe,
for you give us food to sustain our lives and make our
hearts glad; through Jesus Christ our Lord. Amen.*

—THE BOOK OF COMMON PRAYER

A Good Impression at a Dinner Party

THE SOUP SHOULD BE PLACED ON THE TABLE FIRST. ALL WELL-ORDERED DINNERS BEGIN WITH SOUP, WHETHER IN SUMMER OR WINTER. THE LADY OF THE HOUSE SHOULD HELP IT, AND SEND IT ROUND WITHOUT ASKING EACH INDIVIDUAL IN TURN. IT IS AS MUCH AN UNDERSTOOD THING AS THE BREAD BESIDE EACH PLATE, AND THOSE WHO DO NOT CHOOSE IT ARE ALWAYS AT LIBERTY TO LEAVE IT UNTASTED.

YOU SHOULD NEVER ASK FOR A SECOND SUPPLY OF EITHER SOUP OR FISH; IT DELAYS THE NEXT COURSE, AND KEEPS THE TABLE WAITING.

AS SOON AS YOU ARE HELPED, BEGIN TO EAT; OR, IF THE VIANDS ARE TOO HOT FOR YOUR PALATE, TAKE UP YOUR KNIFE AND FORK AND APPEAR TO BEGIN. TO WAIT FOR OTHERS IS NOT ONLY OLD-FASHIONED, BUT ILL-BRED.

IN EATING ASPARAGUS, IT IS WELL TO OBSERVE WHAT OTHERS DO, AND ACT ACCORDINGLY. SOME VERY WELL-BRED PEOPLE EAT IT WITH THE FINGERS; OTHERS CUT OFF THE HEADS, AND CONVEY THEM TO THE MOUTH UPON THE FORK. IT WOULD BE DIFFICULT TO SAY WHICH IS THE MORE CORRECT.

IT IS WISE NEVER TO PARTAKE OF ANY DISH WITHOUT KNOWING OF WHAT INGREDIENTS IT IS COMPOSED. YOU CAN ALWAYS ASK THE SERVANT WHO HANDS IT TO YOU, AND YOU THEREBY AVOID ALL DANGER OF HAVING TO COMMIT THE IMPOLITENESS OF LEAVING IT, AND SHOWING THAT YOU DO NOT APPROVE OF IT.

BE CAREFUL NEVER TO TASTE SOUPS OR PUDDINGS TILL YOU ARE SURE THEY ARE SUFFICIENTLY COOL; AS, BY DISREGARDING THIS CAUTION, YOU MAY BE COMPELLED TO SWALLOW WHAT IS DANGEROUSLY HOT, OR BE DRIVEN TO THE UNPARDONABLE ALTERNATIVE OF RETURNING IT TO YOUR PLATE.

Chapter Eight
DRESSED IN FINERY

*How charming she looked when she came down
on a sunny Sunday morning, well-dressed and well-humoured...*

—CHARLOTTE BRONTË, *VILLETTE*

Her wardrobe, extensive. Her skirts and hats and boots, of the latest fashion. The color and style of her garments, flattering to her face and figure. The Victorian lady knows the importance of dressing right and proper for each occasion. She seldom finds herself underdressed or over-dressed, as she carefully chooses just the right type of gown and accessories for garden parties and balls, household breakfasts and jaunts on her bicycle.

The Victorian lady's closet is filled with an amazing variety of dresses for all sorts of activities.

Dresses in flannel, muslin, or linen for walking, traveling, riding, and ice skating. Dresses for golf, lawn tennis, and even dresses for bathing. And, of course, the delicately-tinted tea gowns and the breathtaking formal gowns for parties and balls, fashioned from fabrics with regal names like organdy, dimity, crepe, satin, and lace, and colored in the jewel tones of violet, emerald, and dark crimson. Underneath her dresses go the petticoats, bustles, corsets, crinolines, and long-trailing skirts that turn young ladies into princesses and mothers into queens.

*A true lady is always
faultlessly neat.
No richness of dress in
the afternoon,
no diamonds in the evening
can atone for unbrushed hair,
a soiled collar, or untidy slippers
at breakfast!*

—*THE ETIQUETTE OF DRESS*

Good clothes open all doors.

—THOMAS FULLER

Her toilette would be not quite finished, of course, without the lavish ornaments and trimmings she selects. Onto her hands go her gloves, satin and lace or soft doeskin, depending upon the occasion. Her feet slip into the finest of shoes—heeled pumps with ribbons and bows, or corseted boots with long, slender laces. She brings out the jewelry box to choose brooches and pendants, bracelets and earrings—diamonds and pearls, or coral and cameos. Onto her head she lightly fastens a straw or organdy bonnet, or, if the event calls for it, an elaborate picture hat topped with feathers and flowers. And then there are the extras—fans and parasols, muffs and shawls.

Anne took the dress and looked at it in reverent silence. Oh, how pretty it was—a lovely soft brown gloria with all the gloss of silk; a skirt with dainty frills and shirrings; a waist elaborately pintucked in the most fashionable way, and a little ruffle of filmy lace at the neck. But the sleeves—they were the crowning glory! Long elbow cuffs, and above them two beautiful puffs divided by rows of shirring and bows of brown silk ribbon.

—L.M. MONTGOMERY, *ANNE OF GREEN GABLES*

What Should I Wear?

❋ Walking Dress—

*With the correct costume a lady may
enjoy the pleasures of a walk in a muddy lane.*

In a town, according to the time of the day, or time of the year,
a walking dress should be simple, yet there should still
be some degree of richness in the dress.

In the country, the attire should be tasteful, solid and strong. The
bonnet may still be becoming though plain, perhaps of straw or whalebone.

Cloaks of a light material for summer, and stout in the winter,
are more elegant and suitable than shawls which belong rather to the carriage or visiting dress. With warm cloak, looped dress, shady hat and soft
gloves to complete a country walking costume, the high-born lady may
enjoy the privileges which her inferiors already possess—she may take a
good walk with pleasure and safety, and not shudder at the muddy lane!

❋ Riding Dress—

Too long a skirt is apt to alarm the horses!

Compactness and utility are the requisites for the riding dress;
and, whilst touching on this point, let us impress strongly the
danger arising from too long a skirt in the riding-habit.

Too long a skirt is apt not only to alarm the horses,
but to entangle, in case of accidents, their fair riders!

As far as a riding costume is concerned, nothing secures the freshness
of the face better than the slouched hat. It is cool, and permits the free
circulation of air around the face, while it protects the eyes, the
forehead, and almost the chin, from scorching heat or withering blasts!

❋ The Carriage or Visiting Dress—

The carriage or visiting dress should be exceedingly handsome.

The visiting dress should be gayer in color,
richer in texture than the morning dress at home.

In summer all should be light, cool, agreeable to think of,
pleasant to look at.

Nothing can be in worse taste than to keep on the warm
clothing of winter, after winter and even spring have gone.

Light scarves in muslin are especially elegant. Delicate silks
are infinitely more suitable to summer and its bright hours,
than the heavy cashmeres and velvets, be they ever so handsome.

❧ DRESS FOR AFTERNOON PARTIES—
Occasions when a woman may feel some hesitation.

ALTHOUGH THE RULES ABOUT THE ETIQUETTE OF DRESS ARE SO SIMPLE, THERE
ARE OCCASIONS ON WHICH A WOMAN MAY BE EXCUSED FOR FEELING SOME HESITATION.

HOSTESSES, ANXIOUS TO PROVIDE SOME NOVEL ENTERTAINMENT, SEND OUT INVITATIONS
WHICH CAN OFTEN PLUNGE THEIR RECIPIENTS INTO A STATE OF EMBARRASSMENT.

NO-ONE WHO HAS EVER BEEN EITHER OVER-DRESSED OR UNDER-DRESSED
AT AN AFTERNOON PARTY IS EVER LIKELY TO FORGET IT!

TO BE SUITABLY DRESSED IS WORTH BESTOWING SOME THOUGHT UPON, PARTICULARLY
IF YOU RECEIVE AN INVITATION, THE HOURS BEING BETWEEN THREE TIL SEVEN.

IN ALL SUCH CASES THE RULE IS CLEAR—AS LONG AS THE HOURS SPECIFIED ARE BEFORE SEVEN,
IT IS PLAIN THAT EVENING DRESS CANNOT BE REQUIRED.

❧ EVENING COSTUME AT HOME
There is something in exposing the bare shoulders and arms to the glare of day, that startles an observer!

PEOPLE IN SOCIETY ARE SUPPOSED TO DRESS FOR DINNER,
AND WHEREVER THEY GO AFTERWARDS THEY ARE NATURALLY IN EVENING DRESS.

THE DINNER HOUR GOVERNS SOCIETY AS FAR AS THE ETIQUETTE OF DRESS IS CONCERNED.

THE ORDINARY EVENING COSTUME AT HOME ADMITS OF GREAT TASTE AND
BECOMINGNESS. IN SOME GREAT HOUSES IT DIFFERS LITTLE FROM THAT ASSUMED
AT LARGE DINNER PARTIES, EXCEPT THAT ORNAMENTS ARE LESS WORN.

A LOW DRESS IS FAR THE MOST BECOMING, ACCORDING TO AGE, COMPLEXION,
AND THE STYLE OF THE HOUSE—A POINT ALWAYS TO BE TAKEN INTO CONSIDERATION.
YET A LADY SHOULD RESTRICT THIS TO DINNERS BY CANDLE LIGHT.

IN SUMMER A THIN HIGH DRESS, AT ANY RATE, IS MORE CONVENIENT AND MORE MODEST.

FOR ALL OCCASIONS A LADY OF RANK AND FORTUNE SHOULD HAVE HER SEPARATE DRESSES.
SHE SHOULD NOT WEAR OUT HER OLD BALL OR DINNER DRESSES BY HER FIRESIDE AT HOME
AND IN INTIMATE CIRCLES. THEY ALWAYS HAVE A TAWDRY, MISERABLE LOOK.

NOTHING IS SO VULGAR AS FINERY OUT OF PLACE!

THE FULL DINNER-DRESS DEMANDS GREAT SPLENDOR. THE DRESS MAY BE BLUE, SILVER-GREY,
MAIZE, LAVENDER, OR (BUT RARE) VERY PALE GREEN; PINK IS SUITABLE ALONE TO BALLS.

THE DINNER DRESSES THAT LAST FOR EVER ARE DETESTABLE!

❧ BALL DRESSES
The lighter and more ethereal-looking the fabric, the more successful a ball dress will be.

THE GREAT POINT TO BE AIMED AT IN A BALL DRESS IS TO GET SOMETHING THAT WILL LOOK
STRIKING ON ENTERING THE ROOM AND YET LOOK NEAT WHEN LEAVING IT.

BALL GOWNS SHOULD ALWAYS BE OF LIGHT DELICATE COLORS,
THE SOFT FLIMSY MATERIALS SUCH AS CHIFFON, NINON AND NET BEING
THE PRETTIEST AND THE MOST GRACEFUL FOR THESE OCCASIONS.

THE GLOVES WORN WITH THESE GOWNS ARE EXTREMELY, LONG, COVERING
THE WHOLE OF THE ARM; AND SHOES AND STOCKINGS WORN TO MATCH.

—THE ETIQUETTE OF DRESS

Some Helpful Hints About Dress

LIGHT AND INEXPENSIVE MATERIALS ARE FITTEST FOR MORNING WEAR; DARK SILK DRESSES FOR THE PROMENADE OR CARRIAGE; AND LOW DRESSES OF RICH OR TRANSPARENT STUFFS FOR THE DINNER AND BALL. A YOUNG LADY CANNOT DRESS WITH TOO MUCH SIMPLICITY IN THE EARLY PART OF THE DAY. A MORNING DRESS OF SOME SIMPLE MATERIAL, AND DELICATE WHOLE COLOR, WITH COLLAR AND CUFFS OF SPOTLESS LINEN, IS, PERHAPS, THE MOST BECOMING AND ELEGANT OF MORNING TOILETTES.

RICH COLORS HARMONIZE WITH RICH BRUNETTE COMPLEXIONS AND DARK HAIR. DELICATE COLORS ARE THE MOST SUITABLE FOR DELICATE AND FRAGILE STYLES OF BEAUTY. VERY YOUNG LADIES ARE NEVER SO SUITABLY ATTIRED AS IN WHITE. LADIES WHO DANCE SHOULD WEAR DRESSES OF LIGHT AND DIAPHANOUS MATERIALS, SUCH AS TULLE, GAUZE, CREPE, NET, ETC., OVER COLORED SILK SLIPS. SILK DRESSES ARE NOT SUITABLE FOR DANCING. A MARRIED LADY WHO DANCES ONLY A FEW QUADRILLES MAY WEAR A *DÉCOLLETÉ* SILK DRESS WITH PROPRIETY.

WELL-MADE SHOES, WHATEVER THEIR COLOR OR MATERIAL, AND FAULTLESS GLOVES, ARE INDISPENSABLE TO THE EFFECT OF A BALL-ROOM TOILETTE.

MUCH JEWELRY IS OUT OF PLACE IN A BALL-ROOM. BEAUTIFUL FLOWERS, WHETHER NATURAL OR ARTIFICIAL, ARE THE LOVELIEST ORNAMENTS THAT A LADY CAN WEAR ON THESE OCCASIONS.

THERE IS AS MUCH PROPRIETY TO BE OBSERVED IN THE WEARING OF JEWELRY AS IN THE WEARING OF DRESSES. DIAMONDS, PEARLS, RUBIES, AND ALL TRANSPARENT PRECIOUS STONES, BELONG TO EVENING DRESS, AND SHOULD ON NO ACCOUNT BE WORN BEFORE DINNER. IN THE MORNING LET YOUR RINGS BE OF THE MORE SIMPLE AND MASSIVE KIND; WEAR NO BRACELETS; AND LIMIT YOUR JEWELRY TO A GOOD BROOCH, GOLD CHAIN, AND WATCH. YOUR DIAMONDS AND PEARLS WOULD BE AS MUCH OUT OF PLACE DURING THE MORNING AS A LOW DRESS, OR A WREATH.

NEVER BE SEEN IN THE STREET WITHOUT GLOVES. YOUR GLOVES SHOULD FIT TO THE LAST DEGREE OF PERFECTION.

—COLLIER'S *CYCLOPEDIA OF SOCIAL AND COMMERCIAL INFORMATION*

*She laid a few ferns and roses for herself,
and quickly made up the rest in dainty bouquets
for the breasts, hair, or skirts of her friends.*

—LOUISA MAY ALCOTT, *LITTLE WOMEN*

Next she turns the attention to her face and hair. She uses little cosmetics on her face, for a naturally rosy complexion is most admired. Her hair is combed and brushed, polished and arranged, sometimes plaited or curled, and put up with hairpins into a tasteful style to complement her dress and jewels. Then come the decorative hair ornaments, feathers and jewels, but she is careful not to use too many. All done up in finery, she is ready to make her entrance!

"Pull out that frill a little more—so; here, let me tie your sash; now for your slippers. I'm going to braid your hair in two thick braids, and tie them half-way up with big white bows—no, don't pull out a single curl over your forehead—just have the soft part. There is no way you do your hair suits you so well, Anne, and Mrs. Allan says you look like a Madonna when you part it so. I shall fasten this little white house rose just behind your ear."

—L.M. MONTGOMERY, *ANNE OF GREEN GABLES*

There were brushes and combs on the dressing-table, scent, and powder.... A satin dressing gown lay on a chair, and a pair of bedroom slippers beneath.

—DAPHNE *du* MAURIER, *REBECCA*

"Young ladies should take care of themselves. Young ladies are delicate plants.... My dear, did you change your stockings?"

—JANE AUSTEN, *EMMA*

A Victorian Face

A VICTORIAN LADY'S VANITY TABLE SHOULD BE WELL SUPPLIED WITH IDEAL COSMETICS FOR CREATING A ROSY, WHOLESOME FACE, AND TO MAKE HER HAIR SHINING AND BRIGHT—

COLD CREAMS *and* LIP SALVES

SILVER NATURAL-BRISTLE BRUSHES

TOILET POWDER *and* FACE POWDER

SOAP *and* WATER

SPONGES *and* BRUSHES

TO KEEP HERSELF LOOKING HER BEST DURING BALLS AND PARTIES, SHE MUST RELY UPON THE TRICKS OF PINCHING HER CHEEKS AND BITING HER LIPS FOR DELICATE COLOR.

Chapter Nine
AWAY WE GO ON HOLIDAY!

To slip down stairs through all the sleepy house,
As mute as any dream there, and escape
As a soul from the body, out of doors,—
Glide through the shrubberies, drop into the lane,
And wander on the hills an hour or two,
Then back again before the house should stir.

—ELIZABETH BARRETT BROWNING

Deep green meadows and heathered hills of the countryside. The invigorating air of the seashore. The excitement of a journey to a never-before-seen landscape, or to a faraway country where customs are new and life is a bit like being in a dream. These are the pleasures of holiday, relaxing and inspiring jaunts that give the Victorian lady new ideas and renewed perspective.

Summertime, oh, summertime, pattern of life indelible,
the fadeproof lake, the woods unshatterable...

—E.B. WHITE

One summer might bring the grand tour—to Europe or the Americas, perhaps, or to take in the beauty of Africa. And of course there are the frequent visits to the seashore, summer after summer. English ladies often favor the South of France, with its delicate breezes and delicious seascapes. An American lady may accompany her family to the summer house on Cape Cod, which is outfitted in white wicker and ocean colors, with plenty of shells and interesting pieces of sea glass scattered round, calling out happy echoes of summers past. Or she may relax in a gracious resort overlooking the water, where her every need is attended to and each day passes in regal luxury.

"To-morrow we shall go to the seaside!"

—THE VELVETEEN RABBIT

We had a most amusing day at Dover on Saturday. The weather was glorious and very hot. Even at the sea there was hardly a breath of wind.

—LADY EMILY LUTYENS, A BLESSED GIRL

Both spring and summer are ideal months to steal away to the country, where storybook cottages and gardens soothe and refresh the lady traveler. In the countryside she takes long walks on the hills, gathering flowers for the tea table and sampling the peaches and apples that dot the orchards. Here she pens her innermost thoughts in her journal, sketching the winding brooks and delightfully funny animals—cows and horses, chickens and cats. Perhaps she lounges in a hammock during hot summer afternoons, sipping lemonade and eating strawberries while lost in a favorite novel, *Pride and Prejudice*, or, say, *Vanity Fair*.

Golden Rules of Etiquette for Travel by Boat and Rail

LADIES WILL NOT PERMIT THEIR ESCORTS *to* ENTER *any* APARTMENT RESERVED *for* LADIES ONLY.

LADIES TRAVELING ALONE SHOULD CONSULT CONDUCTORS *or* CAPTAINS. LADIES WILL THANK GENTLEMEN WHO RAISE *or* LOWER WINDOWS, COLDLY BUT POLITELY.

IF *a* PERSON CRUSHES *or* CROWDS YOU, *and* APOLOGIZES, ACCEPT *the* APOLOGY BY *a* COLD BOW.

GENTLEMEN ESCORTS MUST PAY *the* MOST DELICATE *and* EARNEST CARE *to the* LADY *or* LADIES UNDER THEIR CARE. THE ATTENTION MUST BE UNREMITTING.

AT *a* HOTEL, *the* ESCORT MUST SEE *to* EVERYTHING, ROOMS, ETC., ETC.

COURTESIES *in* TRAVELING *are* ALWAYS *EN RÈGLE*, BUT THERE MUST BE NO ATTEMPT *at* FAMILIARITY.

GENTLEMEN WILL COMMENCE CONVERSATIONS.

GENTLEMEN WILL ASSIST LADIES *to* ALIGHT *from the* CARS.

A GENTLEMAN MAY OFFER *to* ESCORT *a* LADY *to the* REFRESHMENT SALOON.

A GENTLEMAN MAY OFFER HIS NEWSPAPER.

—COLLIER'S CYCLOPEDIA OF SOCIAL AND COMMERCIAL INFORMATION

Fine Dress in the Country

The same dress is worn until five o'clock tea!

DAY DRESS IN THE COUNTRY IS GENERALLY CONSIDERABLY PLAINER. THERE IS NOT THE SAME NECESSITY FOR A CHANGE OF ATTIRE IN THE AFTERNOON AS THERE IS IN TOWN. THERE IS NO OCCASION TO DISCARD THE MORNING TOILETTE AT LUNCHEON. THE SAME DRESS IS GENERALLY WORN UNTIL FIVE O'CLOCK TEA, WHEN A TEA-GOWN IS GENERALLY ADOPTED DURING THE FEW HOURS THAT ARE SPENT IN THE BOUDOIR BEFORE DRESSING FOR DINNER.

WELL-BRED PERSONS DO NOT MAKE AN ELABORATE TOILETTE IN THE DAYTIME IN THE COUNTRY UNLESS THERE IS SOME REASON FOR IT!

—*THE ETIQUETTE OF DRESS*

I am in such a state of happiness I hardly know what to do with myself. Now I am in the country I wonder how I could ever have endured London. The weather is divine, hot, with a delicious breeze. The country looking lovely beyond description and the house and village and everything seems more perfect than I expected it to be....All the rooms here are perfection, but mine is the most perfect of all. It has three large windows and is beautifully light. I have a lovely view and can see the sunset.

—LADY EMILY LUTYENS, *A BLESSED GIRL*

Autumn holidays bring their own special pleasures—camping and hiking trips, and weekends at lakeside resorts. The Victorian lady will dress warmly for these adventures, taking special care to pack cozy flannel undergarments, sturdy boots, toasty hats and scarves, and warm woolen skirts and jackets.

Bags packed, plans made, spirit of adventure propelling her forward, she is ready for her journey. It's time to go on holiday!

Proper Etiquette for a Guest at a Friend's Country House

A visitor is bound by the laws of social intercourse to conform in all respects to the habits of the house. In order to do this effectually, she should inquire, or cause her personal servant to inquire, what those habits are. To keep your friend's breakfast on the table till a late hour; to delay the dinner by want of punctuality; to accept other invitations, and treat his house as if it were merely a hotel to be slept in; or to keep the family up till unwonted hours, are alike evidence of a want of good feeling and good-breeding.

At breakfast and lunch absolute punctuality is not imperative; but a visitor should avoid being always the last to appear at table.

No order of precedence is observed at either breakfast or luncheon. Persons take their seats as they come in, and, having exchanged their morning salutations, begin to eat without waiting for the rest of the party.

If letters are delivered to you at breakfast or luncheon, you may read them by asking permission from the lady who presides at the urn.

Always hold yourself at the disposal of those in whose house you are visiting. If they propose to ride, drive, walk, or otherwise occupy the day, you may take it for granted that these plans are made with reference to your enjoyment. You should, therefore, receive them with cheerfulness, enter into them with alacrity, and do your best to seem pleased, and be pleased, by the efforts which your friends make to entertain you.

You should never take a book from the library to your own room without requesting permission to borrow it. When it is lent, you should take every care that it sustains no injury while in your possession, and should cover it, if necessary.

A guest should endeavor to amuse herself as much as possible, and not be continually dependent on her hosts for entertainment. She should remember that, however welcome she may be, she is not always wanted.

A visitor should avoid giving unnecessary trouble to the servants of the house.

The signal for retiring to rest is generally given by the appearance of the servant with wine, water, and biscuits, where a late dinner hour is observed and suppers are not the custom. This is the last refreshment of the evening, and the visitor will do well to rise and wish good night shortly after it has been partaken of by the family.

—Collier's cyclopedia of Social and Commercial Information

Chapter Ten

WE WISH YOU A MERRY CHRISTMAS

The Holly and the Ivy,

When they are both full grown

Of all the trees that are in the wood,

The Holly bears the crown.

—TRADITIONAL CAROL

Mistletoe dangles from the ceiling of the entry hall, welcoming callers with a mirthful laugh. In the parlor, the Christmas tree shows off its grand ornaments, and children sit underneath its boughs, counting the days, the hours, till Santa arrives with a sleigh full of gifts. Mince pies, plum puddings, and roasted chestnuts make their way in and out of the kitchen, bringing good cheer to the home's merry visitors. Through all this hustle and bustle, the Victorian lady embraces the season with a smile and a heart filled with gratitude. Tis the season for celebration and love, laughter and gaiety. Tis the season of Christmas.

"God bless us every one!" said Tiny Tim, the last of all.

—CHARLES DICKENS, *A CHRISTMAS CAROL*

Perhaps the first thing you'll notice about her gingerbread home brought to life like a *Nutcracker* dream is the decorations. The center of entertainment throughout the year, the parlor steps up its role for the holiday season. A glittering tree claims a prominent place in the room, and under it sit the tempting gifts, wrapped in colorful paper and tied with taffeta ribbons. Some stand out even more with the addition of fine flowers and greenery. Colored glass lamps and candles throughout the room cast a festive glow. The fire blazes merrily, and stockings bulging with gifts and treats dangle on the mantel, while an army of toy soldiers marches above. The fragrance of cedar boughs drifts throughout the house, and arrangements of holly and ivy bring the peace of the winter woods indoors.

Christmas is here,
Merry old Christmas,
Gift-bearing, heart-touching,
Joy-bringing Christmas,
Day of grand memories,
King of the year!

—WASHINGTON IRVING

Beloved Christmas Stories

The Night Before Christmas
CLEMENT CLARKE MOORE

A Christmas Carol
CHARLES DICKENS

The Gift of the Magi
O. HENRY

The Christmas Story as told in the Gospel of Luke

AND IT CAME TO PASS, AS THE ANGELS WERE GONE AWAY FROM THEM INTO HEAVEN, THE SHEPHERDS SAID TO ONE ANOTHER, LET US NOW GO EVEN UNTO BETHLEHEM, AND SEE THIS THING WHICH IS COME TO PASS.... AND THEY CAME WITH HASTE, AND FOUND MARY, AND JOSEPH, AND THE BABE LYING IN A MANGER.

THE GOSPEL OF LUKE

A Victorian Christmas Tree

THE VICTORIAN CHRISTMAS TREE TRANSFORMS THE PARLOR INTO AN ENCHANTED WINTER WONDERLAND. SOME FESTIVE DECORATIONS FOR THE TREE INCLUDE—

GARLANDS *of* CRANBERRIES *and* POPCORN

TINSEL *and* PAPER CHAINS

PAPER *and* LACE ORNAMENTS

TISSUE-PAPER SNOWFLAKES

GLITTERING GLASS BALLS

ANGELS, FAIRIES, *and* SANTAS

AN ANGEL *or* STAR *on the* TREETOP

CANDLES

Besides outfitting her home for the holidays, the Victorian lady also helps decorate the village church each Christmas with boughs of greens and ornament-and-gift-laden trees. She and other ladies will adorn the church tree with clothes and toys for the less fortunate, giving the gift of the season to wee children with shabby wraps and grateful eyes. For this is the spirit of the very first Christmas. Later, perhaps that very evening, she and her husband will bundle up their little ones for the church Christmas service. Whether they travel by carriage across snowy fields or briskly walk several city blocks, accompanied on their journey by dancing snowflakes, their hearts fill with excitement and thanksgiving as they reflect upon the miracle of the season.

Heap on more wood!—the wind is chill;
But let it whistle as it will,
We'll keep our Christmas merry still.

—SIR WALTER SCOTT

Christmas brings the best party season of the year, with dances and sleigh rides through the snow and trips to the big city. The ladies bring out their best velvet and lace dresses for the Christmas ball, and the dances always seem to last a bit longer and sparkle a bit brighter during this season. And the food! Hot roast beef, drumsticks of turkey, hot and cold puddings, port-soaked Stilton cheese, roasted chestnuts, and sweets for the young. So much to anticipate!

The whole sky was blue;
And the thick flakes floating at a pause
Were but frost knots on an airy gauze,
With the sun shining through.

—ROBERT FROST

Caroling parties draw friends young and old, voices blending in harmony to sing the favorite choruses—"We Three Kings," "O Little Town of Bethlehem," "It Came Upon the Midnight Clear," and, of course, a reverent rendition of "Silent Night." This is the season of Christmas, and there's no better way to usher out the year.

Pluck me holly
Leaf and berry
For the day when
I make merry.

—CHRISTINA ROSSETTI

Provisions for a Winter Feast

FISH
COD, CRABS, EELS, GUDGEONS, HALIBUT, LOBSTERS, OYSTERS, PERCH, PIKE, SALMON, SHRIMPS, SMELTS, STURGEON.

MEAT
BEEF, HOUSE-LAMB, MUTTON, PORK, VEAL, DOE-VENISON.

POULTRY *and* GAME
CAPONS, CHICKENS, DUCKS, FOWLS, GEESE, GUINEA-FOWL, HARES, LARKS, PARTRIDGES, PEA-FOWL, PHEASANTS, PIGEONS, RABBITS, SNIPES, TURKEY, WILD DUCKS, WOODCOCK.

VEGETABLES
BEETS, CABBAGES, CARROTS, CELERY, HERBS OF ALL SORTS, LETTUCE, ONIONS, PARSNIPS, POTATOES, SALAD, SPINACH, TURNIPS.

FRUIT *and* NUTS
APPLES, CHESTNUTS, HAZEL-NUTS.

—COLLIER'S CYCLOPEDIA OF SOCIAL AND COMMERCIAL INFORMATION

Such dinings, such dancings, such conjurings,
such blind-man's-bluffings, such kissings-out of old years
and kissing-ins of new ones.

—CHARLES DICKENS

I now have my house full for the Christmas holidays,
which I trust you also keep up in the good old style.
Wishing a merry Christmas and a happy New Year to you and yours.

—WASHINGTON IRVING

The rooms were very still while the pages were softly turned
and the winter sunshine crept in to touch the bright heads
and serious faces with a Christmas greeting.

—LOUISA MAY ALCOTT, *LITTLE WOMEN*

Today in the town of David a Savior has been born to you;
he is Christ the Lord.

—THE GOSPEL OF LUKE

Peace and goodwill, goodwill and peace,
Peace and goodwill, to all mankind.

—ALFRED, LORD TENNYSON

Conclusion

Putting on the most magnificent ball of the season.
Cultivating an abundant garden of old-fashioned flowers and herbs.
Venturing off to a cozy yet fashionable beach retreat to lift the spirits.
To modern ladies, the Victorian lady's life might seem a bit
difficult to emulate in this hectic day and age.

But, if you look at her activities and accomplishments individually—each
one comprised of small sparks of the imagination—they do seem manageable,
some even easy. And they carry with them the promise of rewarding peace,
renewed friendships, and refreshment of soul.

You might sow forget-me-not and columbine seeds in a small
patch of the garden, or pluck a spring of fresh lavender from a modest
box of herbs. You could cut out a simple row of paper dolls with daughters or
little friends, or venture off on a bicycle, with a simple picnic and wool
blanket tucked in a backpack. You can hunt for one-of-a-kind seashells
on the beach, or wander through a city arboretum, journal
and sketching pencils tucked in a pocket.

After all, the timeless beauty of the Victorian lady is
the beauty of her heart.